SCARRED

Scarred by Life. Healed by Scars

KIM LITTLE-HICKS

WESTBOW
PRESS®
A DIVISION OF THOMAS NELSON
& ZONDERVAN

WestBow Press books may be ordered through booksellers or by contacting:

WestBow Press
A Division of Thomas Nelson & Zondervan
1663 Liberty Drive
Bloomington, IN 47403
www.westbowpress.com
844-714-3454

ISBN: 978-1-9736-9678-0 (sc)
ISBN: 978-1-9736-9677-3 (e)

Library of Congress Control Number: 2020912968

Print information available on the last page.

WestBow Press rev. date: 08/07/2020

CONTENTS

DEDICATION

This book is dedicated In Memory of My Little Brother
Alvin SCOTT Little
09-18-1969 / 05-17-2020

Today is Thursday, May 21, 2020. It's taken me a couple of days, lots of prayer, and strength only the good Lord can provide to sit back down at this keyboard and write this dedication.

Four weeks ago, my brother called on his way home from work, seeing his face show up on my cell when he called was ALWAYS a bright spot in my day. "Sis, he said, When is your book coming out? I can't wait to read about myself". And then burst into laughter.

Sharing the process with him of the steps and where we were at that particular time, his response was ahhhh, well, I can't wait."

Never in my wildest imagination did I ever think he wouldn't be here to read this book. To read about himself, to share in the excitement that FINALLY this book is finished after it's beginning nine years ago.

To know Scott, was to know love, kindness, gentleness, laughter to it's fullest. Hundreds knew him as Dr. Scott. Many, many knew him as their friend, he was Dad, to my niece and nephew, and every friend they brought to his house, a 2nd Dad. He loved to give of himself, and the shirt off his back if needed. His patients adored him. His nieces thought he was the coolest Uncle around. He was loyal, dedicated and a magnificent light that God blessed with wisdom, and the ability to comfort all of us on our worse days.

He was my hero, my confidant, my right arm, half of my heart and gone way too soon.

There isn't enough space, or words to begin to describe the depth of pain inside that he's no longer a phone call away. Just to hear his voice I ache for. To hear that laugh, I crave.

Yet, to know he's in Heaven is knowing Heaven is even brighter, sweeter, and more beautiful than ever.

I can only imagine my precious little brother. And I will see you again. Until then, Fly High Bub, FLY HIGH!!!!

"We are confident, yes, well pleased rather to be absent from the body and present with the Lord." 2 Corinthians 5:8 (NKJ)

Scarred by Life....Healed by Scars

CHAPTER 1

The Struggle Inside

Life can really throw some hard curve balls our way when we least expect them.

Actually, there are times we may "think" we're prepared for some of these, yet when reality hits, we are so taken aback, we're left shaking our heads with thoughts of what, why?

Let's travel back to the year of 2011. In all honesty, not a year that brings a boat load of joy with it.

It was a year full of turmoil, strife, belittling, worry, fear, and walking on egg shells.

And it just wasn't in my home life, but my work life, and my Dad on a down hill slope from the effects of diabetes taking a toll on his body, a quadruple by-pass, high blood pressure, amputation of toes, that left him wheelchair bound, and dialysis three times per week.

The struggle inside as an adult child, wanting to take care of your parent, and having two daughters, a husband and a job and being 45 miles away, was exhausting and a total battle in this mind.

You have to work! You have to take care of your children! Yet, your Dad, is alone. Not one single mili-second did the mind rest. But oh, ol slu foot…aka Satan, shoots his firey darts at us where he sees us at our weakest. And at this particular time, it was my mind.

> *"For we do not wrestle aganist flesh and blood, but aganist principalities, aganist powers, aganist the rulers of the darkness of this age, against the spirit hosts of wickedness in the heavenly places." Ephesians 6:12 (NKJV)*

You see, my parents were divorced in 1981 and my Father never remarried.

As January 2011 came, with it Dad's health began to take on even more battles than a body would ever imagine.

Dad, was not a giant in stature. But, a Hercules in strength. He worked hard all his life and he fought hard when it came to battling his illnesses.

There were so many medications, for all the different medical issues, and each carried side effects that would frustrate him to no end.

Having to deal with his blood pressure sky rocketing to stroke levels from one medication, then take another one and his diabetes go through the roof, or get so low it would send him in to panic and anxiety. And believe me, this is just a small glance into what he endured.

Even though he had been confined to his wheelchair for quite some time, he still managed to somehow look healthy for the most part and have to tell his jokes.

His favorite all time thing to do in life was make somebody laugh.

And having to watch his body grow weaker, and color change, and the zeal of trying to bring laughter stale. It was clear Dad was growing weak and weary.

Dad and I had one of those relationships, where I knew he loved me, even without saying it.

He wasn't one to show or verbalize his feelings with my younger brother and I.

Growing up, Dad worked the evening shift at the Mines, (yes, I am a Proud Coal Miner's daughter) so as my little brother and I would be getting home from school, we'd just miss Dad as he had headed for work.

CHAPTER 2

Dealing with Divorced Parents

Actually, Dad and I never had a one on one relationship until my parents divorced. At that time, I was an adult child, married with an eigtht month old baby girl of my own.

Our very first one on one conversations consisted of "You tell your Mother this" and then her going well, "You tell your Dad, this".

To the length and extent panic and anxiety was hitting me and I let out a BIG SCREAM, Tell Each Other Yourselves!!!! I am NOT your guys personal message delivery service.

The mili-second that scream and those words rolled off my toungue, the first thought that crossed my mind was, OH NO, I'm a dead duck!

But as you can see, I lived to tell the story!

That first year of my marriage, having a baby, dealing with my parents divorce was unbelievable stress.

I had no clue what a panic attack was. I just knew, I couldn't swollow, get a good deep breath, heart racing, arm numb and tingling and that my time was short here on earth. Or so it definitely felt that way.

I hadn't given my life to Christ yet, but I sure was prayin'.

And as sure as the sun came up the next day, something would happen between my parents, be it where my little brother was going to live, or how dividing his time between them was going to take place. Would custody be 50/50 or what?

I was a twenty year old my brother nine, and as I would rock my baby girl to sleep or dance her to sleep is what we actually did. My thoughts were we can just keep him too, can't we baby girl?

Knowing how hard this divorce was on a twenty year old, there was no way on God's green earth did I want my little brother having to deal with it.

The only way I could figure to "rescue" him was weekends. And I made sure I got him every weekend. And jam packed as much fun music and anything possible to get our minds off this horrible divorce. Even feeding cows, chickens and pigs at my then in-law's farm.

Whatever it took, though a farm girl I am not. That's what we'd do.

CHAPTER 3

ACOD

My entire life to that point, I'd never been exposed to an ACOD. (Adult Child of Divorce). It felt like Lord Help Me Jesus!

As years past and I had given my life to Christ. Publishing a FREE Christian News Magazine was a dream come true.

During those years, my Dad helped distribute them to serveral different locations in the Left Beaver area where I grew up.

I would later learn, not only was he helping distribute them, he was also reading them from front to back. Glory to God!!!

This hard shell on the outside, man's man began to soften on the inside.

Every single evening at 7PM my phone would ring, it was Dad and he was ready for us to watch Funniest Home Video's together via phone.

Some evenings it was so clear to hear the weakness in his voice. And though he'd try to shrug it off, he was ok, I knew better.

It took him but just a little while before he would call and say, Pray Kim, Pray!

My response, Always Dad, Always!

As tears would trickle down my face, I couldn't began to break out in prayer with him right there on the phone.

The stiffness in my body, every muscle so tense so tight, it felt if I were to move in the least, I would break, the fear of not being able to pray the right words, it was as if I was at a loss of how to pray.

And that would make me so angry at myself. Praying for others was as easy as snapping your fingers for me. So why, Why Could I NOT Pray For My Dad? I repeatedly asked myself and God that question.

CHAPTER 4

Praying for Dad

Then during one of Dad's hospitalizations there we were, just the two of us. Dad always wanted my brother there, he's a PA-C., and according to Dad knew more than any doctor he'd ever seen.

But, my brother wasn't the only one he wanted during these hospitalizations. His sisters he wanted by his side too, and boy were they.

They took such good care of Dad, doting so much time, love and attention. There is no way, my brother nor I could have gone through all Dad did without them.

Still, this particular occasion arose, and it was just the two of us in his hospital room. He was growing weaker, his breaths were becoming shorter, the machines he was hooked up too making those noises that just make your skin crawl. His color was looking like an ashy kind of grey and as I stood by his bedside he looks up at me and says, Pray Kim Pray.

There wasn't time to think about what words or worry if they would be right. Immediately I took his hand and for the first time began to Pray out loud with and for my Dad.

The prayer flowed so easily from my lips, the words were coming from the depths of my soul and most importantly from God's Word.

That was years and years ago, and to share with you the amazing feeling inside of me to stand by my Father's bedside and pray out loud, well, words simply can't describe it.

There was never any hesitation to pray for my Dad from that moment on, Praise the Lord! Now, listen to this, Dad's color began to return as his cheeks got that hint of pink, his breathing began to calm and return to normal, his machines beep, beep, beeping began to grow more silent.

Dad looks at me with this big grin on his face and says, "You got a hot line to the big man upstairs". I smiled back at him, and pointed to the Heavens and said, It's all to HIS Glory Dad, All to HIS Glory!

CHAPTER 5

Care-Giving Genes

My brother got all the care-giving genes. Not me. When it came to hospitals they went hand in hand with anxiety for me. The heart-ache seeing patients in room after room through the halls. Some with visitors, some alone. The overwhelming feeling of helplessness would consume my every fiber. Hives would pop out on my chest, neck, and arms, sometimes to the point I'd look as though I'd been caught in a wasp's nest.

My ever so loving, kind, compassionate little brother knew his big sister couldn't handle these situations alone and would always try and make sure someone would be there with Dad as well as myself.

God love him.

The only other time after years upon years of hospitalizations with Dad, that we would find ourselves just the two of us, happened to be his last night with us.

My brother, bless his heart had been called in the wee hours of the morning to come to Dad's dialysis treatment center. There were complications one after another, and as stated earlier Dad, wanted Bub to be there, and the treatment facility called for him to come.

As my brother was by Dad's side as his Doctors, nurses, entire staff worked diligently, I was enroute to West Virginia for a training session with my job.

Just as a co-worker and myself arrived and sat our computers up, note pads and pens and cells on silent upon our table, and the meeting is about to begin, my cell starts humming and vibrating on the table.

Looking at it, there was my brother's face and I immediately knew something wasn't right.

Grabbing the cell, and making a mad dash just outside the conference room doors, I answered quietly and softly, Hello, Bub what's wrong?

He says, Sis, it's Dad and he's not good. He is enroute to the ER by ambulance and he will be in ICU.

He asked if we had made it to the meeting yet, and said he was sorry but I needed to head to the hospital.

Having carpooled with my co-worker and always so very thankful for her driving, this day I was extremely Thankful to have her.

To begin to tell you the number of times during Dad's surgeries, infections, and many other instances of hospitalizations my brother and I were told he would not make it is countless.

He would fight like no other every single time and prove them wrong.

For me, it was God giving Dad another chance every time to ask

HIM into his heart. To say the sinners prayer, so no matter how against the odds his conditions may have been he came through.

This time not only could I hear in the tone of my brothers voice, I knew this time was different than all the rest.

I knew it deep, deep down in my soul.

CHAPTER 6

Dad's Salvation

Weeks before this last attack on Dad's body, the church I was attending had been praying feverently for him. It was a Sunday after a particular service, Pastor and his wife asked if we could go visit Dad at his house. Of course we can, immediately came out of my mouth with total excitement.

During my years at this church, my church family had stood and agreed with me in prayer and praise for Dad for years. They prayed when I was to weak to pray. Never will I ever forget a single one of them, ever.

Dad, loved company. Still, I called to make sure he was up to having a visit from us before we pulled out of the parking lot. Of course, he said. Come on Up.

The three of us loaded up in their van and headed out for our visit.

Pastor and his wife, had never been to Dad's before this day. On our way I was picturing Dad getting all his knives out, all his coins, and having his collections ready to show and tell them all about them.

Once we arrived, Dad met us at the door in his wheelchair. That once strong body now confined, weak and worn and pale, got an entire different countenance about him. Introductions took place, and the next words uttered, was Dad explaining to Pastor and his wife, follow me, as he led us to the back room where all his collections were. Do I know my Dad or what?

Now Pastor seemed to be enjoying each and every story behind every gun, every coin, every hat, every piece of Dad's collection. God Bless Him.

As hours had passed, the stories changed from subject to subject to Jesus.

Pastor, asks Dad "Alvin, before we leave is it ok with you if we pray"?

Dad answered, "Absolutely"!

Pastor then asked, "have you said the sinner's prayer?" Though not a word was uttered but only through the eyes, the three of us knew Dad wasn't completely sure if he had done what he had needed. Pastor then says, I tell you what, let's pray and you can repeat me after me, is that ok"? Dad shakes his head yes, with a tear falling down his cheek.

As I sat on the end of Dad's bed, one hand holding tightly to his, the other to Pastor's wife. Tears streaming down my face, Praise and Thankfulness screaming from my insides yet silently on the out. Glory to God, I was being blessed to witness my stern, keep his feelings to himself, Dad ask Jesus into his heart.

Pastor began, and Dad repeated every word, and with each word began to sob.

"Dear God,

I know I am a sinner, and I ask your forgivenes. I believe Jesus Christ is Your Son. I believe that He died for my sin and that You raised Him to Life. I want to trust Him as my Savior and follow Him as Lord, from this day forward. Father, guide my life and help me to do Your will. I pray this in the Name of Jesus.

Amen

Well, I was ready to jump a pew had there been one in the room. What exhileration. How Awesome, what an amazing day, Oh what a blessing to witness. Absolutely one of the happiest days in my life.

Leaving Dad's, we said our goodbye's and got our hugs out on the porch. Filled with such excitement to get in touch with my little brother I was skipping down the sidewalk, holding my cell in the air looking for enough of those little signal bars to get a call out.

Everything you have just read to this point, was being played out in my mind like a movie, during the drive back from West Virginia.

Step by step, every moment saved in time.

Having no idea of what all had taken place during this drive, Dad's condition, what all he was having to go thorough. I was just so thankful I wasn't alone.

The next thing I remembered it was as if I had been picked up from that conference room table and placed in the Intensive Care Unit where

Dad layed hooked up to machines, as my brother and family stood by his bedside.

Listenting to the nurses and doctors as they would explain there was nothing more they could do for Dad, hearing his groans and seeing his body jerk in pain the feelings of helplessness were consuming me.

I looked over at my little brother, his eyes so weak and tired from being up hours without sleep and rest. He and Dad's physicians had tried every possible avenue they knew to get Dad transferred.

He needed to be somewhere there were multiple specialists for each complication going on in his body.

Unfortunately, there were none. Not only was there not a hospital with the multiple physicians available, the fact remained Dad couldn't have surrvived the transfer by ambulance or Medical Flight.

CHAPTER 7

God's Amazing Grace

Dad's body had grown septic. The morphine being pumped into his body to try and help ease his horrendous pain, only settled and calmed him for minutes at a time.

Evening came, and family and friends were departing giving my brother and I hugs, love and letting us know Dad and all of us would be in their prayers.

Once Bub and I were alone and had some time to talk ourselves, I pleaded with him to go home, get some sleep and try to rest. He was exhausted. This was his reply, "Sis, are you sure, I know how you are, I don't want them having to work on you too if anything happens, with his sheepish grin. I assured him I would be fine, go get some rest.

To me he is still my little brother, even though he towers over me in height, and at this particular time was 42 years old.

Convinced all would be well, or so I thought, he turns and heads out of the ICU room only to stop directly ahead at the Nurse's station.

This is what I hear, "hey guys, I'm so sorry to bother you all, but

I'm getting ready to head home and try and get some sleep, and my sister is going to be here with Dad." (You also need to know between the two of us we knew all the nursing staff and physicians in ICU. It's a small town.) They're all like, no problem, you go and get some sleep. Bub continues, "You all have no clue how nervous, and upset my sister gets, she has anxiety and if anything were to happen, you guys would have both of them to work on, I'm telling you she'll be passed out in the floor." Here's my cell, just call me, I'm close by and will be here really quick." They all chuckle.

Have to admit it warmed my heart, even though the chuckle was at my expense. He was telling them the truth.

The time was approximately 7:30 ish, and there we were, Dad and I alone in his ICU room. The nurses coming in checking and of course answering my questions.

"Isn't there anything at all he can have to help ease his pain?" One nurse explained, "Kim, honey he is on the maximum amount of morphine a human being can have." In shock, I asked, and he's still awake? She shook her head yes and with compassion rubbed my arm and said I'm sorry honey.

Knowing Dad was in excruciating pain because of his groans, thrashing his body against the railing, eyes looking straight up and squenched when he'd try somehow to relieve the pain. I'd stand by his bedside and comb his hair with my fingers. He started saying, I love you Kim, and I'd say I love you too, Dad. He began to go in and out of consciousness but would ask, "Are you by yourself, Kim?" Yes,

Dad, it's just us I'd say and we're ok. This went on for hours upon hours.

3 AM Dad seemed to be calming more so than he had the entire night.

There was a recliner type chair in the room, so I sat down snuggled up and closed my eyes and began to pray again.

My prayer changed by this time. Now, I was asking JESUS to please not let Dad suffer any more. I talked to JESUS just like I'm writing to you now. As if HE didn't already know, I wanted to assure HIM that my brother and I would be ok if HE took Dad home. We knew he wouldn't be in pain anymore. We knew that wheelchair would be gone and Dad would be walking the streets of gold in Heaven.

It seemed as though it had only been about 5 minutes at the most. Dad began groaning and the groans were more intense. He began thrashing his body more intense, he was jerking. He was trying to mumble something, and I could not make out the words. I just knew his pain was unbearable.

At his bedside, combing his hair with my fingers again, I begin to sing very softly and very quietly the beautiful lyrics of John Newton, Amazing Grace.

My tears were falling onto Dad's pillow as I whispered, Amazing Grace, how sweet the sound, that saved a wretch like me. I once was lost but now I'm found, was blind but now I see, then I asked God, Lord, I beg you don't let him suffer anymore. Barely able to catch my breath, sobbing I continued, T'was Grace that taught my heart to fear,

And Grace my fear relieved. How precious did that Grace appear the hour I first believed.

That instant, the heart monitor flatlined! Noises I've never heard before seemed so loud, Nurses, Doctors, coming from every direction. CODE BLUE, CODE BLUE, I heard over the intercom. Kim leave, go to the waiting area, I heard as they were doing chest compressions on Dad. Stay with us Alvin, Stay with us, I could not move. It was as if I had frozen in time, my footing was froze. I didn't want to disobey the instruction to go to the waiting area. I simply couldn't move. Finally, I caught a deep breath, but felt I was outside my body making my way to the waiting area.

Absolutely the most unusual feeling I had ever had in my life. Finding myself in the waiting area alone, it hit me. God had given me the peace and calmness only HE can give. His Word says, in John Chapter 4 verse 7 (NKJV).

> "and the Peace of God, which surpasses all understanding,
> will guard your hearts and minds through Christ Jesus."

And God had done just that at the exact time I needed HIM most.

I began to Praise HIM as my body walked in slow motion to the corridor of the Intensive Care Unit, where my cell was able to have service. I looked up at what seemed to be this HUGE black and white clock and the time was 5:00 AM. I dialed my brother's cell and he answered immediately, "What's wrong Sis"?

I said, "Bub, Dad has flatlined and they are in there working on him now." He said. "I'll be right there".

The next few hours were a blurr. God had indeed taken Dad home. No more pain, no more thrashing his body, no more wheelchair, no more dialysis.

I don't remember the drive home from the hospital. All I know is I got home. The hours and days ahead were filled with so many emotions it truly is hard to put into words.

CHAPTER 8

Stages of Grief

There are books beyond books and pamphlets that describe the different stages one may go through after losing a loved one.

And most describe or agree there are 5 stages of dealing with grief.

There is anger, denial, depression, guilt and acceptance.

And let me tell ya, none of us will go through these stages at the same time, or particular order listed above.

We are all individually uniquely and wonderfully made by JESUS CHRIST.

Some may experience all five stages, some three, or four. Our experience, our emotions are just the same, our own and as individual as it is natural.

CHAPTER 9

Losing a Parent

Losing a parent will bring a multitude of memories flashing through the mind, one after another. Some bringing smiles along with feelings of warmth to the heart. Some bring joy and even laughter that was shared.

Whether the relationship was close or simply an uspoken love the array of emotions will come that is a guarantee.

Had I not had my brother, daughters, family and friends and most importantly my Lord and Savior going through dealing with these different emotions would have been unimaginable.

Weeks after Dad's passing, during driving for work my car started to make an unusal noise. Without hesitation, or thought I pick up my cell and call my Dad.

His phone was ringing and ringing. Looking at the clock to make sure he was home from dialysis, and he should have been, I continued to let it ring. All I had to do is be able to mock the sound the car was making and Dad would be able to tell me what he thought it was and where I needed to take it to be fixed.

I have no idea how long I held on to that cell letting Dad's number ring. All I know is, like the flipping of a light switch my brain clicked, my eyes popped wide open, I gasped for breath and threw that cell phone into the passengers seat and began to hit my steering wheel crying and screaming at myself. WHAT ARE YOU DOING!

It was so second nature, when it came to my car to call Dad. Seek his advice and thoughts on what was wrong, what I needed to do, and where I needed to go. The thing is, it wasn't until that moment I realized Dad really was gone.

He wasn't going to be answering my phone calls anymore.

CHAPTER 10

When It Rains It Pours

The occupation I held during the loss of my Dad, was that of an Account Executive. Which required a lot of travel, meeting and exceeding budget goals and deadlines along with much more.

Three days of bereavement was alloted for an employee for loss of a close realitive, as is the case for the majority of workplaces.

It was a stressful position, without adding the loss of a parent into the situation.

It was a commission based position therefore meeting those budget goals wasn't an option the option was to exceed them for the more you sold the more commission you made.

All while keeping what is best for your client top priority.

Another aspect of this position included collections from clients that may have for one reason or another missed a payment due to various circumstances.

On the first day of my bereavement time, I received a call from the Supervisor at that time, that I needed to collect a payment and follow protocol in order to "keep my job". The day after we burried my Father, this is what I get.

The call came mid morning, it was a rainy, gloomy day, my emotions were all over the chart. I was grieving, sad, weak, hurt, and this added to the hurt in a way all I could do was cry even more when it didn't seem possible.

The pressure to do a job with eyes swelled out of my head, the aggravation at the disrespect to even be asked to do such was unfathomable to me. I'd always heard the old saying, "When it rains it pours", but never experienced it to this extent.

Looking for sympathy, I suppose I tried to express the frustration and audacity to my husband at the particular time.

Did I receive it? NO! More pressure, Yes!

At home I was always pressured to bring in more money. To add to the financial bucket that seemed to have more holes than I could possibly plug, no matter how much I made.

No matter what I done, no matter how many budgets I met or exceeded, nothing I seem to do was good enough for anybody.

There wasn't even a day to grieve for my Dad, to sit in silence and have time with the Lord.

My mind, and body started taking a toll from all the directions firey darts were being thrown.

There was no peace but stress at work. There was definitely no peace in my home life.

The hives began. My neck, back, legs and arms begin to break out in hives the size of 50 cent pieces. My eyes begin to blurr and turn so red the whites would look as though they were as red as a stop sign. When that happened panic was at an all time high. You see, I was born with -10 vision in my right eye, that allowed me to differentiate between light and dark up until my college years. Then everything faded to black in that eye. My heart would race so fast I could feel the pulse in my neck and temples and my insides felt like they were running a 5k. Arms numb, could not swollow it was horrific.

CHAPTER 11

Stress

The episodes with my eyes finally got me to the point of seeing an Optometrist. Episcleritis was the diagnosis and I had never heard of such a word or any clue to what it actually was, just sounded bad. Turns out it is arthritis of the eye. If you have never endured the pain and agony of arthritis I pray you never have to.

The eyes aren't the only part of this body that experiences it.

However, optical migraines became an issue which entailed steroid eye drops, laying in a dark room with a warm compress over the eye or both which ever was occuring at the time. And to top it off, you never knew when one was coming. It happened in the middle of work days, where it was impossible to do what was needed. Just had to pull myself up by the bootstraps, press forward and keep on going.

Stress was a major factor riddling my entire body with aches and pains besides my emotional state.

CHAPTER 12

July 2011

Six months after Dad's passing, our family planned our first family vacation to Myrtle Beach, SC. Something I could get my mind to looking forward to spending time on the beach with my daughters, son-in-law, only grandchild, niece, nephew, brother, and our Mom.

For me, the Ocean is one of the greatest of all God's creations. The Peace that comes from listening to the waves, walking in the sand at night, taking it all in and savoring the moment.

This vacation was going to provide a healing from hurt, loss and rejuvenate me being surrounded by those I love most, that was what I envisioned.

However, it turned out to be nothing like I hoped, planned, or even considered.

The humilation, embarrassment, and taking a time I needed so desperately with my family and turning it into a total nightmare was almost more than I could physically or mentally bear.

Trying so tirelessly each day to put a smile on my face around my family and pretend everything was just peachy wore me out.

This five day vacation felt like years to me. I would lie awake at night crying and praying for a billboard from God that it was ok with HIM for me to get out of this marriage.

My mind could not imagine God wanting me to stay where I definitely wasn't wanted, loved, respected, or treated with a kind word.

I was reprehensible is what I thought.

As I sit here writing this, the picture of a little girl, sitting in a corner, knees to her chest with her arms wrapped around them, head buried in her arms sobbing as she no longer wanted yelled at, no longer wanted cursed at, no longer wanted belittled, but she can't move. She's stuck. Is exactly how I had pictured myself all those years. Not as an adult, not as another's mate, but STUCK.

However, I will share with you though Divorce was exactly what we both wanted and needed. The battle that took place to get it almost took me out.

Mentally, physically and emotionally.

CHAPTER 13

Starting Over at 51

Starting a new life over at the age of fifty-one is scary, shocking, and sad.

Scary, because since the age of nineteen being married is all you've known.

Shocking, because you never really thought you would be beginning again after the age of fifty.

And sad, well, sad because no matter how old your children are, you fear "who" may become a part of their lives next, add an only grandchild to that mix and WOW, you just can't imagine having to deal with sharing that baby.

So, we discussed earlier the stages one goes through after the death of a loved one. Never would I have ever imagined six months later, experiencing some of those same stages going through a divorce.

But why not? Divorce is like death, the only difference is death is final. And as long as you share a child or children with someone, you will have to at some point once again be in the same place at the same time and Pray to God both adults can behave like so.

Here comes the emotional rollercoaster. Get ready, Hold on!

With divorce comes anger. And Paul tells us in the Bible,

> "Be angry but do not sin; do not let the sun go down on your wrath". Eph. 4:26 (NKJV)

This was probably one of the hardest of all to not wollow in, especially when bedtime came and its time to lie down and finally get some sleep, and yet your mind plays out every single action against you, every word against you, its like a movie playing in your head on repeat. Worst of all there is no turn off switch on your head to make those firey darts STOP. And where does ol slu foot aka Satan love to come at us most, our minds, our thoughts, especially at a time he sees its open season. Screaming at the top of your lungs into a pillow, using that same pillow as a punching bag, pulling your hair and pleading with God, please Dear Lord Jesus, wipe my mind clean and free of these memories.

Time passes and you can finally begin to ease and feel the calmness of the Lord and get some rest.

Not sure about those of you that have gone through a divorce after 30 plus years, but this ol girl, could not wait to take back my maiden name.

There was so much denial as to WHO I was. I had totally lost her through the years. And the fear of ever finding her was overwhelming.

I mean I knew my God was not a God of fear, but of love and understanding.

Here I was knowing His Word in my heart, but I couldn't manage to get the heart and the head together.

The other stage most statistics agree on when going through a divorce is grief.

What I grieved most was my grandchild not having his grandparents together. No more Family Thanksgiving gatherings, no more Christmas gatherings, no more Family Unit gatherings.

And then it hit me. What good with that be for my grandchild to grow up having to watch me walk on eggshells for a Thanksgiving or Christmas dinner. SHAKE IT OFF GIRL!!!!!

CHAPTER 14

Moving On

The blessing of a townhouse was available and for the first time in my entire life, I would be living alone. Call it crazy, petty, whatever you may choose. All I knew was NOTHING from my previous life furniture wise was going into my new home. We had agreed everything on the inside of the home I could have. So, out came the cell, pictures were being taken as fast as you could swat a fly.

Got on Social Media and posted, "Going Out of Marriage Sale". It's ok to get a good chuckle there, most did including myself. But hey I thought it was an amazing title to catch attention and that it did.

Forty-five minutes after being on Social Media every piece of furniture sold! Glory to God!!!!

From that sell, it was possible to refurnish the new home with brand new things. It was a lot of fun decorating the new place, changing up the color scheme that had been used previously and just making it my own little nest.

Also, blessed with an entire month of not working and being able to keep my grandson and soak up every giggle, every expression, every single move he made. He was my sunshine on my cloudy days, he lit up like a Christmas tree when we made eye contact. He loved me so unconditionally and filled my fiber with joy. God knew I needed this child in my life more than I could ever have imagined.

That month was providing me restoration. Deciding I needed more wisdom than ever, my morning's began with Proverbs. Proverbs is the book of wisdom. And if there is anything I can pass along to someone going through loss, be it a father, or a marriage it is soak up the WORD. Get yourself into the book of Proverbs daily.

Let the Lord wrap you in His arms of comfort through His WORD when you need comforted most.

This particular month seemed to last a year for me. Usually a month flies by. But, Praise God, not this one.

The process of getting to know who I was - was beginning to take root. Letting go of past hurt was beginning to sprout and this was a journey looked forward to and welcomed with wide - opened arms.

CHAPTER 15

Let the Journey Begin

We're skipping along to the year of 2013. Being in a new career Managing a local clothing store and loving our crew and customers, and seeing all the new clothes, shoes, and jewelry arrive each week was such a blessing. During this time chronic bronchitis landed me in the hospital for a few days on IV antibiotics. We had a huge corporate vist coming in to the store, and there was so much needed done there was absolutely no way I was gonna lie there in that hospital bed and leave all that work on my girls. Sure weakness was apart of this but one's gotta do what one has got to do.

I pleaded with my Dr. to release me explaining every little detail that needed accomplished before our visit with corporate. Relentlessly I might add, for he wasn't agreeing to release me on my first plight.

Finally, after making promise after promise of taking it easy, taking my meds etc., He released me, and Off to work I went.

Rule No. 1 when taking a strong antibiotic that has a label on the bottle that says: Take With Food, one should abide by said label.

Needless to say, the take with food part was skipped because I simply didn't want to take the time to eat.

It's sweltering hot outside, and inside was barely comfortable because of the many windows in the store.

Yet there were displays needed changed above the racks of clothing, close to the ceiling. So the ladder on wheels was pulled out, up that ladder I went with arm draped in the change of clothes for the display and sweat was dropping off me like raindrops. Man, was it hot up there at the top.

Couldn't tell you how long I was actually up there, until I was at the bottom on the floor without taking one step down. Scared us all half to death. But, all was well. Thank You Jesus!!! And mission of getting the store up to par was accomplished.

Don't think my system, my bodily system ever quite regained the strength it once had, because everything began falling apart or so it seemed after.

A few weeks later, opening early alone while walking into the store I glance into one of the glass columns on my way to the back. Stopped in my tracks, took a second look and my lips looked like Donald Ducks they were so swollen, not sure if it was panic/anxiety but again, not being able to swollow occured, I looked at my arms and I was covered in hives. Immediately called my brother, whom was working at a nearby ENT office. What's wrong with me Bub, as I explain my symptoms.

Get here quick, he said. Children, I could not even tell you if there was one Red light on the way to that office, because there was no stopping me from getting there, the swelling was getting worse by the minute. Sure enough, upon arrival, she's having an allergic reaction to antibiotic occurs again, at work and I can't see. The entire store was a total blurr, instantaneously the panic and anxiety set in. I locked it up, and headed straight to the closest eye dr. Afterall, I was behind the wheel and all is a blurr at 20mph.

This time both eyes were experiencing optical migraines and I had to be picked up from the dr.'s office and taken home.

At the follow-up visit I would learn that what I referred to as my good eye, was now no longer 20/20 vision.

I totally felt like Linus in the Charlie Brown cartoons, and there was this gloomy, dirty, dark, of dust following me every where and trying to destroy my health. And it's spelled

S-T-R-E-S-S.

CHAPTER 16

Ramifications

There was more on my plate than any human should have to carry. Dealing with threats, and the phone calls because certain areas of the divorce were not turing out into a particular favor. And here again, everything was my fault. And it wasn't. And no matter how hard I tried to get up, put my face on, curl this head of hair, and go out into the workforce with a smile on my face while my insides were being torn, well, the body feels it.

This ol girl ain't what she used to be, standing 12-14 hrs a day, lifting heavy boxes of shipment, wasn't cutting it for my arthritic, fibromyalgia, bulging and ruptured disc's, anymore. Nope, my family Physician was sending me to more and more specialist and the decision was made to take me off work.

Fifty-three was feeling like ninety-three. My mental state was all over the map.

Depression was at its all time high.

What was I gonna do? How was I gonna make it? Where was I gonna live?

CHAPTER 17

When the Little Brother Becomes
His Big Sisters Rescue

Even starting this chapter the tears are covering the keyboard as I begin to type. From the day my parents brought my baby brother home from the hospital, and told me to sit on the couch as my mother placed this tiny little baby in my nine year old arms, she said, "here you go, here is your very own little live babydoll." Those words were gold to me. I took them seriously, without hesitation, and became his second momma, protector, care-taker, but in my mind, I loved him more than anyone. He was mine!

And he as well as I, had expericed divorce months after losing Dad, and we shared so, so many sleepless, up all nighter talks and we were both broken, and trying endlessly to be supportive and be a rock for one another.

The day I found out my doctor was taking me off work due to the multiple health complications and disablity was going to be the next step for me, he was the first person I called.

At this particular time, he was in search of buying a home in a neighboring county, where his children were enrolled in school. And yet, still very close to his place of employment. As if it were nothing at all, he quickly says, so we'll just look at 4 bedroom houses instead of 3 Sis, you can move in with me, and on the weeks I have the kids, you can help with after school pick up's, getting them to and from extra-cirricular activity practices, and games until I get there after work. How super smart was he? He made me feel needed insead of a burden. My niece and nephew never felt in my heart as a niece and nephew, they felt more like my grandchildren. And to this day are treated as such.

The house was purchased, and here we go moving in on Christmas Eve. Two households into one. We were blessed with such good friends and family to pitch in and get us all in there, set up, and even had a Christmas Tree up all in a 24 hr. timeline. God is So Good!

During the following months my mornings after school drop off's, consisted of doctor appointments after another. Medical bills that were agreed upon in our divorce to be paid, hadn't and collection companies were ringing my cell off. They were piling past the $40,000 range and I was suffocating, with no income to pay any kind of amount. A new - used vehicle had to be purchased when starting the position at the clothing store, and now there was no way to make that payment. Depression, was taking over. And no matter how hard I tried to hide it, I just couldn't anymore. Could not make my face smile, stop the tears, or stop from not wanting to get out of the bed. At night when the kids and my brother were asleep, I would bury my face in my pillow and cry till I couldn't anymore.

Never dreaming they might be able to hear me. Yet they could.

Knowing filing for bankruptcy was inevitible, still I could hear Dad's voice in my head, "Don't ever file for bankruptcy, don't ever own a credit card, if you don't have the money to buy it, then you don't get it." So, in my mind, I drove up to the bank my vehicle was financed through, walked in handed them the keys, and explained how sorry I was, but I could no longer afford to keep the vehicle.

Little did I know, it doesn't work like that. It should, in my opinion but in reality it doesn't. No, you gotta file for bankruptcy and the vehicle has to be repossessed. Seriously, how much more depressing can it get?

Don't ever ask those words, unless you want to find out. Because believe me, you will.

After trying to turn the car in on my own, it was time to find an attorney and proceed with the dreaded Bankruptcy.

The gentleman that was known to be the Best in our area as an attorney for just this situation was exactly the one I turned to.

It was clearly, easily seen within the first fifteen minutes of our first meeting why so many said he was the Best.

He had a heart that truly took interest in your situation and was quick to share encouragement and the ability to make you feel everything was going to be just fine.

When the mounds of paper work, folders upon folders of medical bills and then the vehichle was handed across his desk, he says, "this is it"? At that point I didn't know whether to jump up and down, shout for joy, or smile the biggest smile I could muster.

He had made one of the most difficult days seem so much better. I was truly grateful and thankful.

Upon leaving his office, driving down the street the feeling of disappointing Dad came over me like a big dark black cloud.

Dad, may no longer be here, yet I know he knew what I had just done.

Oh, the overwhelming feeling of disappointment engulfed me.

CHAPTER 18

Unworthy

The deep dark excessive unworthy, useless, despicable human being I was, was as deep inside me as a massive black whole.

Therapist, after therapist reliving every single solitary detail of what brought me to where I was made life full of gloom and despair.

The diagnosis' of PTSD, Severe Depression, Panic and Anxiety were confirmed time and time again with each and every therapist.

Every single time the PTSD diagnosis would come up, my mind would directly go to, but I'm not a Veteran.

Finally, for some reason the third time to hear it, I said those words out loud, instead of in my mind. I am not a veteran. How can I have PTSD, I asked.

Well Kim, when you get upset by things that remind you of what happened in your previous marriage. You're experiencing nightmares, flashbacks, events that make you feel like it's happening all over again. You are emotionally cutting yourself off from others, You feel numb, lost interest in things you used to do and love. You are constantly on guard looking over your back waiting for something bad to happen. You are jumpy, startled, not sleeping, all of which are symptoms of PTSD and can occur in individuals without being a Veteran. All of which were true, but I didn't know.

This along with the debilitating mental disorder that affects your life to the point you feel unworthy and carry such a heavy sadness around all the time, coincides with severe depression.

Take the fact that I wasn't in a church on a consistent basis because there was no energy, nor desire to get out of the bed.

I was a loser, I had lost everything I had worked for the past 31 years. I lost the ability to get out from under debt. I lost who I was.

And the next decision from the Therapist was I needed admitted to help me regain me again.

CHAPTER 19

My Vessel from God

It was mid March the year 2015. My 3rd year of living with my brother. But also my 3rd year out of church regularly.

This weekend though, my brother had gone to Lexington and left me his little UK Blue Convertible BMW to get out of the house, put the top down, and just drive.

It was a Sunday Morning, early to. The sunshine was shinning so bright through my bedroom windows, and I could see the bluest sky from the thin line of separation in the sheers on the window.

I got up, took a shower, put on a face (that's make-up) for those that may not know. Got dressed in jeans and a sweatshirt and headed for the Beemer.

Backing out of the driveway, my thoughts were, ok where am I gonna drive to?

We were living in a county just approximately 15-20 minutes from the one I'd raised my daughters in. The one I called home.

So, turned on the radio, hit the gas and let the wind hit my face and all of the sudden Chris Tomlin came on the radio with their song Good Good Father.

Oh the longing for a church. As I was driving passed our Community College, and taking in the beauty of the rich blue sky, the lush green in the trees and different colors of flowers popping up along the way, I looked to my left and saw a building that said Elevate Church.

There were all kinds of people in the parking lot. Smiling faces and I noticed as they grew closer to the door, they were greeted with hugs instead of handshakes.

That was unusual, really nice I thought. And man I could really use a hug right now.

Elevate, hmmmm what an encouring name I thought. I looked up, and there I was sitting in there parking lot. As if Jesus litterally had taken the wheel and set me there. I began to talk to Him, Lord, why am I here? I don't know anyone here, I can't just walk in there by myself.

Continuing to observe, this had to be the friendliest bunch of people I had ever seen. It was like they truly loved every single soul coming thru those doors.

Before I knew it, the car door was opened, purse on my shoulder and I was walking inside Elevate Church. In Jeans and a Sweatshirt. OHMIGOODNESS!!!!

Standing there was one the most beautiful souls I had ever met. Not just inside, but her outside, man she was and still is beautiful. Long beautiful brown hair, sunkissed skin, a smile like no other with those pearly white teeth, and she stretches out both arms with a big

"Welcome to Elevate" hug, not one of those what I call fake hugs, where you get a little pat on the back, nope, she squeezed me with a big ol bear hug, and said you look so familiar to me, and I love your hair. She said. At that instant it dawned on me my windblown hair had to be all over my head. And I hadn't even thought about it.

Too late now, I was in the door. I told her my name, and it was my first time to visit Elevate.

She said, "Well, Glory to God sister we love having you and you're welcome here anytime, all the time.

Her zest, zeal, smile, unconditional love toward a total stranger, me, now that right there is how I want to be!

As she directed me to the sanctuary I began to think, I hope I don't get anyone's regular seat, that would just be awful. As I looked around I spotted a couple I had once attended another church years ago with.

A couple I love dearly, two of the most anointed Prayer Warriors I have ever been blessed to come into my path. It had been years since seeing them, and I was so tickled they were there. I went straight over to the two of them, and it was as though we had never been apart.

There just happen to be a vacant seat next to this marvelous woman. How thankful I was for that. And those seats were dead center facing the stage.

Soon, the Elevate Praise Team took the stage. When this group began to play and sing God's Praises my entire body was covered in God Bumps (goose bumps to some). Their voices were so strong and beautiful just as I imagine Angels singing. The keyboards were amazing, the guitars man oh man, and then the Drums! Never had I ever experienced Worship on this level that beautiful and Elevating in my life.

As they were about to end, and the Pastor was about to take the stage, this young handsome 22 year old young man steps up and takes a mic.

I thought oh, this one is going to sing. NO.....This young man Opened his mouth with such excitement, encouragement, and elevation as he welcomed everyone to Elevate Church this morning.

I'm looking at my friend, wide eyed and she says you just wait!

Well, he asks we bow our heads as he began to pray over the service.

He asked for God to use him to touch those that need HIM most. He said You Are Welcome Here Holy Spirit, he said we love you, we praise you, we Honor you, in Jesus' Name, everybody said, and there was a roar of AMEN!!! It was electrifying.

The Praise Team began to exit the stage, as this young man began to share; the Title of Today's Message is, "Stop Believing the Lies".

Talking to myself, I'm saying are you kidding me right now? I spent three days in therapy last week listening to my therapist tell me I had to Stop believing the lies that had been spoken over me. And this is his message today. I could feel my entire body shake.

And evidently so could my friend. She reached over took my hand held it in hers, and squeezed it tight.

Pastor began, "Don't you dare children of God let anyone kill steal and destroy your self-worth. That is pure do Satan, roaming arond to see whom he can devour. Well, my eyes were leaking like a water faucet. He continued, "Today it Stops, Right Here, Right Now. God wants you to know You (and then he literally points his finger right at me) are a child of the Most High King. And you are beautifully and wonderfully made. He knew you in your Mother's womb. He knew the number of every hair on your head. Stop, you hear me, STOP believing the lies others have tried to make you believe, lies that have been spoken over you.

I was a sobbing mess! Holding onto my friends hand with the tightest grip I could, laying on her shoulder. No way this Pastor could have known what I was going through. He had never met me. God was using Him, His vessel to get through to me, to Stop wallowing in the degrading, belittling, hateful, hurt to the core of my being words that had been spoke over me for 31 years to the point I had believed them.

I had never felt the presence of God so full in my entire life. The Holy Spirit so strong, I began to look around and it wasn't just me this message was for. There were so many He spoke to that day.

When service was over, I didn't want to leave. I wanted more! It was at that moment I realized I had found my home church.

Throughout my Christian walk, God has blessed tremendously. from 2000-2004 I was able to Publish a Christian Magazine called The Christian Messenger. During those four years, I was blessed to travel the Tri-County area and interview and write Feature articles on various multiple denominations, Pastor's, Praise Teams, And Members that had received Miracles from God!

Fifty -five years in age, a twenty-one year old Born Again Christian, that thought she'd experienced it all, Was in for an entire different realm.

I truly believe there are multiple denominations out there to fit each and everyone of us.

Elevate Church, was my fit. Non - Denominational. Glory to God. Why, because I love all denominations, doesn't matter to me what's over the door. If you're a born again Chrisitian you are my brother or sister in Chirst.

Believing in a one on one relationship with our Savior is my belief and was Elevates. To love unconditonal, to serve, to help and step out of my confort zone to do what Jesus has called us to do and be encouraged to do so.

Elevate, had all walks of life sitting in that congregation. Doctor, Lawyer, Nurses, Recovering Alcoholics, Recovering Drug Addicts, to name a few, and Pastor wanted equal unconditional love and prayer, for all of us.

Its one thing to stand up and say, It doesn't matter what 's on your outside, it what's in your insides that count. It wasn't lip service. To say, Come as You Are. Some dressed to the nines, some unable. But all treated with love and respect.

Yes, the day I walked in the doors of Elevate, I walked in - in a down hill slope emotionally, from betrayal, the loss of my Dad, Divorce after 31 years, taking emotional abuse and losing my home, vehicle, bankruptcy and myself.

I had no idea who I was anymore. 1,838 days of being like a 2x4 beaten into the ground with a sledge hammer getting up and finding me just didn't seem possible anymore.

All the bricks and concrete blocks I carried on my shoulders and back each with a label of how unworthy ugly and undeserving I was, found me at the point of no return.

Until that beautiful March day, I walked into those doors!

God's Not Mad at Me....He's Mad about Me...my Pastor taught me that!

CHAPTER 20

The Great Physician

As 2015 progressed, so did my mental state of mind. Setting my priorities on my Lord Jesus Christ, His Word, involving myself with my new found home church. Life was taking on an entire new journey for me.

Psalm 107:19-21 (ESV)

> "Then they cried to the Lord in their trouble, and he delivered them form their distress. He sent out his word and healed them, and delivered them from their destruction. Let them thank the Lord for his steadfast love, for his wondrous works to the children of man!"

Thank You Lord! Not only could the gloom, despair and agony on me feel lifted. But, those I love most were seeing a difference. A she's baaaaack kind of difference. Glory to God!!!!

2016 came, along with it was time for me to move out of my brother's home and into one of my own.

Preparing to look at possible rental properties, Mom was going through a hard time having to watch her husbands health deteriorate and hear the words most dreaded from his Hospice care that there wouldn't be much time left for him.

She pleaded with me not to rent a place just yet, to wait because if she lost him there was no way she could live alone.

Knowing she was going through so much and not in the best of health herself I didn't want to add any more stress to her, so I postponed the search.

Hospice was correct in their assessment of Mom's husband and only a few months had gone by when he was called to Heaven.

My brother had noticed on his way home from work one day a For Rent sign on a beautiful brick home. He actually remembered the number and we called and set up an appointment time to look at the house.

Mom and I both fell in love with the house. The layout, the space, how the majority of both of our furnishings were going to fit. My major concern was the heat. She froze all the time, while my body's thermostat was on HOT FLASHES 24/7.

Knowing her, and knowing myself this was going to be an issue for us. Along with several others that came into play after we actually made the move together.

Some of the issues were petty and small while others were not.

Leaving home at the age of 19 years old and not living with a parent again until 50 plus is an adjustment. I couldn't help but laugh hysterically when I would want to run to the store for something at 9:00PM and she would try her best to convince me I had no business out on the roads that late, I didn't need whatever it was, it was bedtime. She would get so aggravated because she thought I should eat on her time schedule. And that Hershey Bars with Almonds was NOT A MEAL. They were for me.

She started going to church with me and loved it, as well as everybody there. However, when church was over it was time to go home, eat and take a nap. My standing around afterwards and talking to everyone got on her ever last nerve. She would go to the car, sit and pout and give me the silent treatment on the way home. Every Sunday, until I said, we're going to start driving separate. WHY, she loudly asked. I said because you want to hurry and rush home, eat and take a nap. And I don't. There's no problem with us driving separately Mom, I'd tell her. But she didn't like it one little bit.

Months past, and my youngest daughter (30 plus now) ended up moving in with us as well.

Thank God she did! For not long afterwards, Mom started falling in the middle of the night one to many times. Once she fell in her bathroom and ended up in a fetal position around the toilet between the cabinet of the sink and there was NO WAY I could have gotten her out of that alone. But my daughter did.

The side effects of Mom's medications could cause dizziness. She took the majority of her medications at night with the exception of those needed during daytime hours. We had gotten her a bedside potty chair so that she wouldn't get up in the middle of the night, try to make it to the bathroom and fall.

But, she wasn't using that potty chair and that was that.

This would be the time you would need to insert where the child becomes the parent to their parent.

And the parent was not about to reverse roles. Laugh out Loud!

Mom had a sharp tongue. And I'm not about to tell you she didn't.

She could cut you down and swear on her life she didn't say it.

We butted heads over that so much I think there are still knots in mine.

She had bouts with hospitalizations, and being the one taking her to her appointments and so forth. It was a constant battle when I would explain to the attending physician she was having memory issues, and actions of onset dimentia.

She would pass whatever test they give at three different hospitals for dimentia with flying colors. And take that walker and priss outta there like, take that, told you I didn't have dementia.

So, 3rd time was charm for me. And that's when I told her there was no more "acting" like she couldn't remember things and making me worry sick about her, because we now had three different confirmations she was fine as frog hair.

Oh that woman, she got to the point she would only eat what I would eat, she wanted to wear the same colors to church as me, as close to the same outfit as possible. It didn't matter what I did she wanted to do it too. My daughter got to the point of literally laughing hysterically especially on Sunday mornings when Mom would come in my room and ask what I was going to wear, what color, what shoes etc.,

She was something else.

CHAPTER 21

2017

About to Meet my Boaz

Early Spring of 2017, a friend and guy I had gone out with in High School in the 70's., sent a friend request on Social Media one evening. We caught up with each other for a couple days via messaging back and forth before exchanging telephone numbers.

We realized we had gone through so many simular things throughout our lives and knew exactly how the other felt.

We knew bouts of depression. We knew what divorce felt like, and each stage that came with it. And most importantly we knew neither of us EVER wanted to experience that again.

As time passed and our friendship rekindled we began going for rides on his Purple Harley-Davidson Road King which was Awesome.

He took me to places right here in our back door I never knew existed and the beauty of our majestic mountains with the sun shinning and glistening off the leaves as the wind blows through your hair is magical, and so peaceful as you get to see and think about all the beauty of God's creations.

Of course Mom wasn't liking the fact I was riding on the back of a motorcycle. And there's the one day we rode 300 miles and I should've been home way before I got there. What a hoot!

Well, Boaz means strength is within him, when you look up the meaning of Biblical names on the behindthename.com. On waitingforyourboaz.com means "preparation, it's a time to prepare for wifehood and pray for your future husband and yourself.

Praying for a soulmate I was. I wanted a Godly man, that put God first. That would worship, serve and praise God with me. That treated me with respect. That loved me just as I am. My faults, freckles and most of all my faith. I prayed for an equally yoked, Boaz and the wisdom to know him when God put him in my path.

And the more we talked, the more we shared. The visiting one another's church's. My friend sure was starting to look a lot like my Boaz.

Then the more we talked, the more he would visit, the more Mom would talk to my daughter and others how she wanted to get a place of her own. She wanted to check out a nearby place where there were more people her age. This place had church on Tuesday nights, and different types of classes, just everything one would need on sight.

When I would ask her about it, she would say, well if you end up getting married that's where I'd want to go. But, you don't need to get married again you need to listen to me.

That was hard for me to do, and she knew it. Why? Because Mom had been married 4 times so, I was kinda like uh, really? I asked her if she thought I didn't deserve a chance at happiness. I'm only 57 (that is the new 47 today right?). She'd get all fidgetity and red faced and get up and go take a nap. When I was trying to get a chuckle outta her.

It was Sunday morning where my Boaz's parents go to church and he had asked me go with him. After the service, and everyone is standing up to leave, my tall, dark, blue-eyed handsome Boaz with his hands on my shoulders, leans down to my ear, and says I love you!

Children, there was more butterflies in my stomach than there is butterfly species in Peru and that's 3,700.

I was like did he really just say that. Or did I want him to say that and imagined it. Now what do I do? Wait and see if he says it again? But if he did say it and I don't say it back, that's hurtful. OHMIGOODNESS, what do I do?

Forget the new 47 thing, I've just traveled back to 17. Lord help me!

Thankfully, on the way back home he looks over at me and says, did you hear what I told you back at church. Eeeeeek!!!!!! He did say it! He did say, I love you!!! So, I explained what I just shared with you and then said, I am so glad because I love you too!!! Ahhhhhh! Ain't that just the sweetest?

Months go by, one Sunday he went to his church and I went to mine but he was picking me up afterwards to go to Lexington. I was thinking Red Lobster here we come. Love Red Lobster, those garlic buttery biscuits, and Lobster and Crab legs dipped in all that buttery goodness. My mouth was about to slap my brain out just thinkin' about it.

It was absolutely pouring the rain that Sunday and instead of pulling into Red Lobster. He pulled in at Jared's.

I kid you not, the man took me to Jared's. As in Jared's Jewelers

We walk in that amazing jewelry story so eloquent looking like two drown ducks. Glory be to God, this was the exact location one of my dearest friends worked at and she imediately comes to give me a hug.

Grinning from ear to ear, she says and what can I do for you guys?

Boaz proceeds to tell her, we need to look at some rings. Long story short, in all my excitement and totally forgetting Lobster by now, we pick out 3 different rings. I refused to choose, wanting him to so I went outside and found a little awning to stand under while he made the choice.

My friend was just as excited as I was. Which made it even better. They motion for me to come back in, she pulls a little chair out for me to sit in, and my Boaz got down on one knee, asked me to marry him and placed the most gorgeous ring ever, on my finger.

Of course I said YES!!!

CHAPTER 22

Icing on the Cake

After we arrived back home, I could not wait to show Mom the ring. She was quite giddy and happy and thought it was gorgeous. And I was so relieved and happy she did.

Next morning sitting on the back porch in my happy place (the swing) Mom comes out with her ring on. "Let's see who has the biggest diamond", she said. I come back, Mother, you are kidding me right? She wasn't she thought it was fun to compare them. Okay.

Then she wanted to know if the wedding date had been set, no not yet. Well good, that gives me time to get out of here first she said.

At this point, you just got to laugh, or else you are gonna be crying all the time.

She had planned the entire day out of where all I needed to take her. She had made a list, and we were going to check it off stop by stop. And that is exactly what we did.

First stop was to the place she had decided she wanted to live. She wanted to see if they would let her check out the apartments, and put her on the list for the next available.

We got that done. Checked off the rest of her list and she was ready for home and a nap.

Approximately, an hour later she comes out on the porch to see if I want to go through her shoes since we wore the same size and see if there were any I wanted that she wasn't taking, because she has those packed. PACKED, you're packing?

She never ceased to amaze me. It was going to be a month before an apartment would be available. Here I think she's napping, and she's packing.

The next few weeks flew by, seems to be that way when you're having fun.

My Boaz and I had decided we wanted a very small wedding. So, we decided to have it at church during one of our Wednesday night services, but only a few were in on the fact it would be a wedding instead.

It was perfect. Small, intimate, and walking down the isle with my grandson on one arm and my nephew the other, as my brother stood as my Best Person, and youngest daughter as his Best Person, to God Bless the Broken Road by Rascal Flatts, to my Boaz was the Icing on the Cake.

CHAPTER 23

Dusk till Dawn

The month was November, and we set out making this house a home.

Heard a gazillion times throughout my life, the importance of "date nights" for married couples. Ours began at Lowe's. And picking out paint colors, tiles, you name it and we went full speed ahead. My goal, was to have it all ready by Christmas so we could host our joined family.

And we made it! And what an overwhelming feeling of love it was to have everyone here with us.

As months passed, I continued taking Mom to and from her Dr. appointments. And some months she was loving her new apartment, making friends, and others she would not want to move from the couch.

She had done really well up until June, if I remember correctly. I know it was summer. And there was a picture she wanted hung in her bedroom. After getting her the picture, and taking it down to her apartment I had left behind the hammer and hanging supplies. She was not a happy camper.

Explaining to her not to worry, I would be back the next day to hang the picture for her, she amused me by saying ok.

That evening at dusk, my cell rings from a number I didn't recognize. But for some reason I answered it. Normally do not.

Thank God, one of Mom's frineds, not being able to reach her by phone went down to check on her in her apartment. There laid Mom, blood on her head, forearm, fingers. And her friend explains I need you to get down here fast, your Mom has fallen.

My Boaz and I rush to her apartment, where the EMT's were present for an ambulance had already been called.

Not realizing she wasn't whispering to one of the EMT's she tells him, shhhhh, there's my daughter don't tell her what happened she's gonna be so mad at me.

What have you done Mom, I asked. I had only been home an hour and a half from her apartment. She sheepishly barely whispers, nothing.

Nothing turned out to be she had tried to hang the picture on her bedroom wall, one leg on a flimsy nightstand that was more for looks than holding up a body, and the other leg on the edge of her bed.

While trying to use the handle of a butterknife to hammer with. Oh my heavens to Betsy, I said.

So off to the hospital we go!

This trip took us to three different hospitals. She had landed hitting the back of her neck on the solid wood footboard of her bed. Breaking her neck.

It was the wee hours of the morning, dawn, when she was transferred to Lexington, and the fog was so thick visibility was zero unless one happened to be fortunate to be following another vehicle.

Which was a major blessing for the one of two hours it took me to get there.

Four long days of tests after tests, no sleep, no shower, but washing off with baby wipes and still not sure what the plan was going to be for Mom.

My brother and sister - in - law, were able to relieve me once the work week had ended and stay with Mom.

Being in the Medical field as a PA-C, my brother knows how to talk medical terminology and get things moved along. Glory be to God!

Mom would be sent back here locally to a Nursing Home for a time period of rehabilitation and she could get back to her own surroundings.

Once I received the call from my brother, he was headed to the Nursing Home with Mom. I set out to make her room as homey and pretty as possible. Making sure framed photo's of all her grandchildren and loved ones were placed on the window sill of her room, with a beautiful wreath on her door and brand new comforter and matching sheets, enough pajama's, socks and her favorite snacks all to be there when she arrived.

She was pleasantly surprised but exhausted. And defintely ready to stretch out in her bed and get a nap.

CHAPTER 24

Round 1,199 with Mom

Time served in rehabilitation for Mom was over and she was being released to return to her apartment.

As my brother and I stepped outdoors to talk neither of us thought she should go back to her apartment alone just yet. Not because the physicians were releasing her to early. But, because we both know our Mother and her unwillingness to follow orders be they from physicians or us.

She wanted to do things her own way and over do things when she was having a good day, only to do more damage to herself and feel it the next.

We both thought and pleaded and begged for her to come home with me for just a little while longer before going back to her apartment.

"Absolutely not, she wasn't having it, she wanted to go to her own place and she was perfectly cabable" quote, unquote.

She made it approximately 3-4 weeks, before she called one day and said, "ok I think you need to come and get me, and I'll stay with you for a little while". We were into the end of August of 2018 now.

Off I go to pack up her things and Praise God my Boaz went along.

We set Mom up in the Master Bedroom, with every little possible thing one could think she may need in reach.

She was waited on hand and foot, bathed, hairwashed, nails painted, food carried to her at her beck and call. Whatever she wanted, whatever time she wanted it. I made sure she got it.

Still, she seemed angry. I could over hear her conversations with her siblings, cousins, and a couple friends simply because Mom could not whisper, or talk in a low tone. And the things I was overhearing her say about me, were crushing.

I couldn't understand it, and still don't to this day. Her words like those mentioned before, would not leave my thoughts. I would call my brother and unload on him. My Boaz, God love him, he got to watch and hear it all. And when I would cry from the sting of Mom's tongue he would cry for me.

One evening my brother called to say he was going to run up and visit. I went into tell Mom, Bub is going to come up after he gets off work this evening to see you. She threw those covers off her, sat up in the bed and said, "help me take a shower". The shower was perfect in the Master bath for it has a built in seat. I could move the nozzle in the exact position needed to help her. As I was shampooing her hair, she looks up at me, looks around the bathroom and says, ya know this is a beautiful bathroom, I love the colors. I said, Thanks Mom. She said, but you shouldn't be the one to have it, you don't deserve this big beautiful home, I do. The SHOCK on my face had to be crazy, because my mouth felt like it hit the floor. So I shook my head and told myself snap out of it, she didn't mean that, she's joking.

So I began to laugh and said Mom, you crack me up you are so funny.

She says, well I don't know why I'm not trying to be.

I could feel my entire body tense up. I could feel the onset of a panic attack. Trying to keep myself composed and not end up in a puddle in the floor. Got her a towel, and helped her into the bedroom. She wanted her overnight bag that contained the clothes she had brought and were still in. She asked me to go so she could get dressed. I said I need to help you. She said NO, I want to do it myself, go.

Getting to the couch, I was taking deep breaths and praying. Lord Jesus, I need YOUR strength. I need the peace Your Word says surpasses all understanding. I am not understanding this Lord. Help Me!!!

It wasn't very long, and my brother pulls in. I got up to go let Mom know he was here.

The look on her face, was the look of total disgust. I remember thinking, why in the world do you look so disgusted your favorite child is here. Bub, was the apple of Mom's eye. He was her pride. His visit, I thought would light her up like the Northern Stars.

Didn't take long before knowing what that look was all about.

Bub, could tell I had been crying, and he and Mom both sat down in the loveseat at the same time. Only she was at the edge of the seat, facing him.

So, he lovingly pats on her and says, how you doing Mom, you're looking pretty with your make-up on, hair curled, and all dressed up.

And Mom begins...

"You need to take me to my apartment now. I hate it here, she don't feed me, pay attention to me, I might as well not even be here and I sure don't want to be. " I'm looking at Bub, he's looking at me, I couldn't hold the tears back another mili-second. I said, that is it! I am done. My brother, looks at Mom, and says what are you doing? Why are you saying these things Mom. As if Sis isn't even in the room knowing better. She crossed her arms and man was she mad.

Bub, told her she owed me an aology right now. She said, oh no I don't take me to my apartment and I mean now.

He began to tear up, and shake his head and kept repeating Sis, I am so sorry. I told him he owed me no apology whatsoever, but please take her to her apartment I couldn't take anymore. I was at the dry-heaving stage of crying and in total disbelief my mother just said all she did.

My Boaz was out on the riding mower cutting grass and was oblivious to what was taking place.

I got up, went to the bedroom and was packing Mom's things so fast it was as if I were a tornado. I picked up her bags, her potty chair, every single solitary item she had and carried it all out while my brother was helping her into his car.

I took the load to his trunk, once Mom was seatbelted in, he shut her door and came back to me. There we stood in tears, both of us. Who is she? My brother kept trying to console me, and convince me it was the side effects of Mom's medications. She didn't feel that way about me, she loves you Sis you know that. I am so sorry. I fell into his chest sobbing. And told him I would be ok. Just take her to where she wants to be. And they pulled out of our diveway.

For five years, YES five, it took for me to heal from the words spoken over me, the lies I believed. And finally, God had renewed my mind. HE had given me rejuveation. HE had made it possible to restore me, to believe I was capable of being loved and deserved to be. HE had given me back the years that were stolen.

Joel 2:25 (NKJV)

> "I will restore to you the years that the swarming locust has eaten, The crawling locust, The consuming locust, and the chewing locust, My great army which I sent among you."

And this with Mom, had triggered it all back. Different person. My Mother. It did not matter that I knew everything she was saying about me wasn't true. The pain was excuriating.

It's my Mom for crying out loud.

My brother got her to her apartment and called once he had gotten home. He said she acted like nothing ever happened. She was tickled pink to be back in her apartment and I wasn't mentioned along the way there.

Still, I wasn't able to talk just cry and not understand why.

The following weeks, my daughters, grandson, brother, niece and nephew were picking up where I had to stop. There was no way I could go back into that dark whole of depression. There was no way I could accept Mom's sharp tongue and let go of all she had said. I was praying for her, mightily. It was just a time I had to regroup and regain again ya know?

I would call her landline and cell to check on her. Most of the time she wouldn't answer me. And when she did the conversations were short, and to the point. I had to depend on my daughters, niece, nephew and brother to give me the full download on Mom. Which continued to be good days and days not so good.

CHAPTER 25

The Call

It was Friday, September 28th around 11ish AM, a call comes on my cell with the name of the apartment complex where Mom lived. Figured maybe she had locked herself out of the apartment while going downstairs (via elevator) to check her mail.

No, that wasn't it at all. It was a call to inform me that Mom had fallen.

I asked, if she was ok, where she was and definitely wasn't prepared for what would come next. She explained the ambulance, was there and I needed to get there. The minute we hung up, my brother calls, I can hear in his voice this was bad. He said, Sis Mom fell off her balcony. She landed face down, they are transporting her to Pikeville and it's not good.

My husband and I were almost at the turnoff toward Pikeville, my entire being was ripped to shreds. Mom was on the 3rd floor of the complex. So, simply guessing at this point I was having to imagine her falling 20-25 ft. to the ground.

We all make it to the Emergency Room. She was trying to talk a little bit and only every other word could be understood.

It was a warm beautiful day. And Mom had windchimes she was trying to hang on a nail of the awning over her balcony. All 99 pounds of her 5ft. tall body had taken a wire clothes hanger, hung the chimes over the hanger and would stand back and try to jump a little to get the top part of the hanger over the nail. The hanger was stretched into one thin line. We would find out from a resident later that evening.

As my brother consulted with surgeons and physicians just outside the room. He motioned for me to come with him. There he told me, there was nothing they could do for Mom. Every bone she had was broken and she was bleeding internally.

The next hours are blurry, but trying to remember, she was moved upstairs to a room.

My Pastor, our families and friends were all coming to be there with us. We knew Mom wasn't going to make it, we just didn't know how long. In my mind it would be days. Not hours. My firstborn was at the head of the bed near Mom. She could hear Mom saying, I fly way. So she asked her if she wanted to hear the song I'll Fly Away. Mom got a yes out, and my daughter pulled up the song on her cell, played it and Mom would hum.

When it was over, Mom said, again. And the song was played again, not a dry eye in the room. I was standing at the foot of her bed and having experienced being in the room with three other loved ones that had passed, I lifted Mom's sheets to see blue feet. I knew it wouldn't be long.

At 7:00 PM Mom was taken home to Heaven.

CHAPTER 26

Step by Step

One of my dearest friends, actually a cousin and Sister in my Heart, had shared with me after losing both her parents she felt as if she were an orphan. No matter how hard I tried to understand that feeling for her, I couldn't. Because at that time I still had Mom.

Leaving that hospital that evening, on our way home it hit me.

Now I could relate. I too have lost both my parents. Now I could understand.

Mom, had for years written every single step exactly how she wanted her funeral. She had her casket picked out, her flowers, her burial spot, she only wanted to be out at the funeral home one evening and burial the next. And she had even Pre-Paid for it all. Years before she passed.

She knew the songs she wanted sang and had added in her instructions my brother and I could choose who we wanted to sing them. She left explicit instructions Capitalized, Underlined, that my brother and myself were the only two to speak at the funeral home.

She wanted my hair-stylist daughter to do her make-up and hair. She wanted white silk pajamas. And our Pastor to speak at the burial.

Everything was done to her specifications, with the exception of locating white silk pajamas in our Tri-County area. And we tried.

We did manage to get as close with cream pajamas with a little lepoard print touch, which suited Mom to a T.

The graveside service was intimate with family only and Mom's brother sang one of the most beautiful songs I've ever heard. Pastor's words were perfect. I do believe Mom approved of her wishes being carried out as she had penned years ahead.

CHAPTER 27

Expected or Unexpected

Death no matter expected or unexpected can absolutely knock the wind out of loved ones.

As we drove away from the cemetary, I can remember thinking wow, wonder how the stages of grief are gonna hit this time.

Losing Mom in a freak accident was totally opposite of losing Dad.

This time anger was the culprit to latch on and keep me on my knees for deliverance.

Angry at myself, because I couldn't make my mind remember a single positive, good word she said to me. Only those last months of taking care of her, and the saltiness she uttered during.

My Aunt, Mom's sister, God love her has spent hours upon hours reminding me of my childhood, how much Mom loved me. Without my Aunt, I didn't have those memories.

Honestly, I think my mind set was taking 10 steps backwards from the deliverance God had given me from all those abrasive, abrupt, aggressive, maddening words spoken over me years and years prior.

No person I could ever think of would ever want to have only hurtful memories. And neither did I.

Photo albums, Mom had taken all the photo's I had accumulated over the years, (I love family pictures) she had put in individual albums per person. And hand wrote little captions underneath or beside of them.

Those have been a total God send to be able to go through and read and see her handwriting.

Then there was the time, I was swinging in the porch swing and I am not kidding you when I say, this HUGE black snake was on the porch rail directly behind me head up and ready to join me in the swing, when Mom came out the storm door, eyes as big as saucers and said, Kimberly Lynn do not move.

Well, I don't care how old you are when your middle name is included from a parent you do what they say.

Next thing I know Mom barrells out the door, NO WALKER, butcher knife in hand, goes to the other end of the swing, grabs that HUGE black snake by the tail (that we in all honesty) thought was a copperhead. Slings it off the porch, goes down three steps, and chops its head off all in less than five minutes.

Not knowing whether to laugh or cry at his point, I did both. All with the cell in hand recording every second.

Take some advice here, do not and I repeat do not post on social media of your 70 plus year old mother killing a black snake unless you want the wrath brought upon you.

There were so many mean as all get out responses over that post I deleted it, and the memory I just shared with you is all that is left of how fast adrenelin can take over the body be it 70 plus and go into protect mode no matter what!

Point being in this chapter, even when our minds are telling us we aren't loved. We are! Actions do prove it, hearts do heal, anger does go away, and God's light shines through once again.

CHAPTER 28

Broken Bones

Now we are skipping into 2019. Life is good even though there are still trials and tribulations to face. We're gonna move into the second week of November, where my husband and I were at the storage building. Fall leaves had covered the yard and bottom step of the four it takes to get up or down from the porch.

As we were leaving, not thinking about that bottom step being covered in wet fall leaves, I go down the steps first only I missed the fourth one, my right ankle turns and CRACK, like the breaking of a tree branch. I hit the ground like a ton of lard. Screaming my head off. Never had broken a bone in my life, but given natural childbirth twice, and I am here to tell you breaking the right distal fibula was worse!

The pain was excruciating, the nausea, dry heaves, what on earth have I done?

Well, trip to the ER and X-ray's and yes definitely broken, Fitted for the boot, and instructions No Weight Bearing for 4-8 weeks.

Can't drive, it's the right leg. During these weeks of elevating the leg and going for follow-up X-ray's my weeks of remaining leg elevated and stay off began to take a toll.

Talking to my firstborn on the phone one evening, well, having a poor pitiful me talk can't walk conversation she quickly pipes up, "Well Mother, you're going to have to learn to knit, or crochet, or do something to pass the time. " I can't even thread a needle let alone knit, or crochet.

But that conversation made me begin to think what could I do that could turn this lemon into lemonade.

Lightbulb went off, asked my Boaz if he would care to look in one of the bookshelves for a leather blue journal. He found it.

Brought it over to me, and wow, did the memories begin to flow.

That journal was intended to be a book, kind of a testimonial if you will, of this whirlwind of emotional rollercoaster life that began spiraling out of imagination nine years ago.

Life happened and that dream of seeing that book to fruition was put on the backburner, or on the second shelf of the bookcase.

Until, knitting, and crocheting wasn't an option while being immobile with a broken distal fibula for 8 weeks. It was time to start writing again.

It has been an experience and a half. Reliving those emotions. There's been days returning back to this keyboard was not even an option it was to raw. Things you think you've gotten over years ago.

But, ya know what, it's been such a healing process as well.

The very first Saturday, being able to drive and get out of the house. Lunch with my brother, niece and nephew was planned.

Oh soaking in the brightness of such a beautiful sun shinny day, window down even though the heat in the car was on, there was a whole new appreciation for blue skies, sunshine, and wind in my hair.

Arrived at the resturant we were meeting at, parked and got outta my car and my right knee sounded like a bowl of Rice Krispies. Snap, Krackle, Pop and out it went.

Grabbed the door handle to keep from hitting the ground. Couldn't let go to search for my cell in the bottomless pit of my purse, to call my brother to come to my aide.

Taking deep breaths, holding onto each car in the lot, taking baby steps, finally made it inside.

Spot my brother and the kids and he says, "Sis, you ok, you look whiter than a ghost".

Needless to say, the pain had taken the appetite. And my brother had to drive me home.

Feeling like one of those bobbleheads you sometimes see in people's back window's of their car, that was me. All I could do was shake my head. This isn't real. It is not happening. My knee did not just go out on the same leg the broken distal fibula was that had me homebound for 8 weeks. Well, sister, sorry to tell ya, but it did happen!

Next thing we were off for X-ray's and while they were at it, they decided to X-ray the knee, the ankle (distal fibula) and the right hip.

Dr. comes in to let us know he can STILL see the break in the ankle, along with a lot of arthritis, the knee does as well have a lot of arthritis but also an injury where an MRI is needed. His office would be scheduling it and contacting me with appointment date and time. Until then, I was to keep my leg elevated and non - weight bearing. If I could include emoji's the one with the girl with the hand over her eyes on her forehead would be inserted here.

CHAPTER 29

Scarred by Life....Healed by Scars

We are now in April 2020 and the date the MRI was scheduled. However, due to the Coronavirus Pandemic, I decided to reschedule and remain home quarantined and homebound as I have been now for 19 weeks.

The lemonade to all this....is that every single trial, tribulation, heartache, pain, confinement and scars that has came my way, this book is the result.

Even though my scars may not have been visible to the human eye. They most definitely were to my Saviors.

HE, was with me every step of the way. And Praise God, continues to be with me today.

And though knowing what HE had to endure for you and me, sends chills up my spine. It is life altering and we should NEVER forget.

Jesus was beaten and lashed. He had a crown of thorns pushed on his head until blood was running down his face, He was made to carry

His cross along the way to the hill where he would be crucified. The crucifixion took place known as Calvary.

Crowds gathered to mourn and watch Jesus' death.

I cannot fathom having to watch Jesus' death.

As Jesus was nailed to the cross between two criminals and His sides pierced by a sword. And while He was mocked, one of the criminals asked Jesus to remember him and Jesus responded:

> "Jesus then looked to heaven and asked God "forgive them, for they know not what they do." Luke 23:34 (NKJV)

You see, Jesus knew from the beginning everything He would have to endure for you and for me.

Every, lash to His back, every betrayl, the crown of thorns to His head, nail scarred hands, wrists, all of it.

So that we could be forgiven of our sins to never be remembered again. To be healed from the scars this life gives. All we have to do is repent, ask Him forgiveness and come into our hearts. To take these scarred tribulations and heal us with the scars He took for us.

If you or a loved one have carried the scars of life and find yourself riddled in despair, depression, anxiety and an overwhelming feeling of worthlessness.

Please learn from the mistakes shared in these pages with you. Don't wallow in your pain. Hide it with a smile. Waste numerous sleepless nights. Lose yourself and disconnect with Jesus.

Run to Him, Soak His Words like a sponge, etch them into your heart. He will never leave you, nor never forsake you.

He is waiting with open arms to engulf you, guide you, direct your path, shower you with the peace His Word says, surpasses all understanding. Fill your every fiber with joy, hope and an uncondtional love like none other. He is the way, the truth and only waiting on you to invite Him into your heart.

If you haven't yet, here is the Sinner's Prayer To Receive Jesus as your Savior.

Lord Jesus, I come to you asking forgiveness of my sins.

I believe with my heart Father that Jesus died on the cross for my sins, that He was raised from the dead on the 3rd day. I ask you Lord to come into my heart this day. And help me to follow you all the days of my life.

"For whoever calls on the name of the Lord shall be saved."
Romans 10:13 (NKJV)

If you prayed this simple but powerful prayer and have given your life to Christ Jesus, please find yourself a Bible believing church, and may God's Blessings, Deliverance, Love, Peace and Joy fill you.

Should you wish to contact
me for discussion or prayer email:
scarredbylife@yahoo.com

SOME FAVORITE SCRIPTURES AND PROMISES OF GOD

(ESV) Eastern Standard Version

2 Peter 1:4 And because of his glory and excellence, he has given us great and precious promises. These are the promises that enable you to share his divine nature and escape the world's corruption caused by human desires.

Jeremiah 29:11 For I know the plans I have for you," says the Lord. "They are plans for good and not for disaster, to give you a future and a hope.

Matthew 11:28-29 "Come to me, all you who are weary and burdened, and I will give you rest. Take my yoke upon you and learn from me, for I am gentle and humble in heart, and you will find rest for your souls.

Isaiah 40:29-31 He gives power to the weak and strength to the powerless. Even youths will become weak and tired, and young men will fall in exhaustion. But those who trust in the Lord will find new strength. They will soar high on wings like eagles. They will run and not grow weary. They will walk and not faint.

Philippians 4:19 And this same God who takes care of me will supply all your needs from his glorious riches, which have been given to us in Christ Jesus.

Romans 8:37-39 No, despite all these things, overwhelming victory is ours through Christ, who loved us. And I am convinced that nothing can ever separate us from God's love. Neither death nor life, neither angels nor demons, neither our fears for today nor our worries about tomorrow—not even the powers of hell can separate us from God's love. No power in the sky above or in the earth below—indeed, nothing in all creation will ever be able to separate us from the love of God that is revealed in Christ Jesus our Lord.

Proverbs 1:33 But all who listen to me will live in peace,untroubled by fear of harm."

John 14:27 "I am leaving you with a gift—peace of mind and heart. And the peace I give is a gift the world cannot give. So don't be troubled or afraid.

Romans 10:9 If you confess with your mouth that Jesus is Lord and believe in your heart that God raised him from the dead, you will be saved.

Romans 6:23 For the wages of sin is death, but the free gift of God is eternal life through Christ Jesus our Lord. The promises of God are powerful and awesome to grasp. I pray that these scriptures about God's Promises help each of you.

Printed in the United States
By Bookmasters